A Day in the Life of a...

Refuse Collector

Carol Watson

Watts Books
London ● New York ● Sydney

Ian is a refuse
collector.
Each morning
he arrives
at the depot
and changes
into his blue
overalls ready
for work.

"Morning, John," Ian says to the driver, as he climbs into the truck. He puts on gloves to protect his hands.

3

Once the team
are on board,
they set out
for their work
area in the
refuse truck.

The driver is in
charge and he
decides which
streets they
will visit first.

The back of the truck is
split into two sections.

The wider section is for
the main rubbish, and the
other section is for waste
that can be recycled.

"I'll start 'pulling up'," says Ian, when they reach their patch. He and the others collect the rubbish and make a pile of bags in the street.

The main rubbish is in big plastic sacks. Things like newspapers, cardboard, bottles and jars are put out in smaller bags.

"We'll start loading now,"
says John. The refuse
collectors make sure the
waste goes into the
correct section of the truck.

Ian presses a
button on the side
of the truck, and
the 'hoppers' pull
the rubbish
upwards and
scoop it all inside.

Meanwhile, at home in her kitchen, Anna is filling a carrier bag with newspapers and jars.

She puts the blue bag outside ready to be collected.

Later that morning, Ian spots the blue carrier bag. "One more bag for recycling," he thinks, and he puts it into the truck.

"OK, lads, the truck's full!"
calls John. "I'll take it to the tip."
While the others continue to
collect rubbish, John drives off.

He takes the truck to the
transfer station where the
main rubbish is emptied into
a huge hole. Then he heads
off to the recycling depot.

At the depot John watches
to make sure that all the
waste in the smaller section
of the truck tips out onto
the ground.

Then a digger truck drives
up. It pushes and lifts the
rubbish onto a conveyor belt
at one end of the depot.

The conveyor belt carries the rubbish up to where 'pickers' are waiting to sort it out for recycling.

One picker pulls out newspaper,
another collects the cardboard,
and others pick out glass,
plastic and cloth.

John drives back to join the others. They work for hours clearing more rubbish from their patch. "That's it," says Ian. "We've finished!"

Back at the depot,
Ian has a shower to
wash off all the dirt
and grime. "I'm ready
for a good meal," he
thinks, and he heads
off for home.

Recycle your rubbish

Many of the things you throw away with your rubbish can be used again to make other things. If you recycle as many waste materials as possible you are helping the environment.

1. Collect empty glass bottles and jars. (These can be green, brown or clear glass.) Remove the lids and rinse the bottles out.

Take them to a bottle bank and make sure you put them in the correct container for their colour.

2. Save metal cans from food, pet food and drinks. Ask an adult to wash the cans out, open both ends properly and stamp on them to flatten them out.

Take them to an ali-bank, save-a-can bank or give them to a recycling centre.

3. Collect comics, magazines and newspapers. Take them to a paper bank.

Don't waste paper. When you are writing or drawing use both sides of the paper.

If you live in an area where your refuse collector takes all these things away, make sure you leave them out **separately** to your rubbish.

How you can help your refuse collectors

1. Put your rubbish out the night before it is due to be collected.

2. Make sure that the bags are sealed up properly so that rubbish does not spill out.

3. Ask an adult to make sure any broken glass, china or other sharp objects are wrapped up well in thick layers of newspaper.

4. Ask an adult to put a cork on the end of needles or syringes that are thrown away.

5. If you live in an area where the refuse collectors take away waste for recycling, make sure it is in a separate bag from the main rubbish. Don't put it in a black bag.

6. Flatten out any cardboard boxes.

Facts about your rubbish

Each home produces about a tonne of waste every year. Every week refuse collectors pick this up and take it to a tip. In this book the tip is called a transfer station.

At the transfer station the refuse trucks empty the rubbish into a large hole. The rubbish is then taken from the hole and put into huge containers. Barges carry these containers down the river to a landfill site, where the rubbish is buried in enormous holes in the ground.

When the holes are full they are covered over and the land is used for grazing animals or sporting activities.

Sometimes the rubbish is burned and the gas it produces is used to make electricity.

It is important to recycle as much refuse as possible as this saves taking more wood, aluminium and other raw materials from the environment. It also reduces the amount of rubbish that has to be buried in the ground.

Index

© 1996 Franklin Watts

Franklin Watts
96 Leonard Street
London
EC2A 4XD

Franklin Watts Australia
14 Mars Road
Lane Cove
NSW 2066

ISBN: 0 7496 2335 7 (hb)
0 7496 3617 3 (pb)

Dewey Decimal Classification
Number: 363.72

10 9 8 7 6 5 4 3 2 1

A CIP catalogue record for
this book is available from the
British Library.

Printed in Malaysia

Editor: Sarah Ridley
Designer: Kirstie Billingham
Photographer: Chris Honeywell
Illustrations: Ian McNee

With thanks to: Bob Read, Head
of Waste Management, Kensington
and Chelsea; Ian Smith, Paul
Steele, John Altree, Richard
Shepherd and other members of
BFI Waste Disposal; Anna
Wethered and Rufus Bellamy.